Help Your Child
with Literacy

Also available from Continuum

Flying Start with Literacy, Ros Bayley and Lynn Broadbent

Foundations of Literacy, Sue Palmer and Lynn Broadbent

Getting the Buggers to Do their Homework, Julian Stern

Parent's Guide to Primary School, Katy Byrne and Harvey McGavin

Help Your Child to Succeed, Bill Lucas and Alistair Smith

Help Your Child to Succeed Toolkit, Bill Lucas and Alistair Smith

Help Your Young Child to Succeed, Ros Bayley, Lynn Broadbent and Debbie Pullinger

Getting Your Little Darlings to Behave, Sue Cowley

Teaching Assistant's Guide to Literacy, Susan Elkin

Teaching Literacy, Fred Sedgwick

Help Your Talented Child, Barry Teare

Help Your Child with Literacy

Caroline Coxon

continuum

Continuum International Publishing Group

The Tower Building, 11 York Road, London SE1 7NX

80 Maiden Lane, Suite 704, New York, NY 10038

www.continuumbooks.com

British Library Cataloguing-in-Publication Data

A catalogue record for this book is available from the British Library.

ISBN: 0-8264-9572-9 (paperback)

Library of Congress Cataloging-in-Publication Data

A catalog record for this book is available from the Library of Congress.

Designed and typeset by Kenneth Burnley, Wirral, Cheshire

Printed and bound in Great Britain by Ashford Colour Press, Gosport, Hampshire

Contents

Introduction

Why is literacy important?

Imagine what your life would be like if you couldn't read and write. Think of all the everyday tasks that would become a struggle, and how difficult it would be to learn anything at all. That's how important literacy is!

Is this the book you're looking for?

Are you the parent or carer of a young child, keen to help with schoolwork at home – keen, but worried that you might not do a good job?

Or, perhaps you're just starting out as a teaching assistant, or you're a person who helps out with reading at the local primary school?

Then read on!

Go into any high-street bookshop and you will find shelves and shelves of workbooks for young children, with a bewildering array of titles and levels. It's sometimes hard to know where to start!

Then, on the TV or in the papers, there's yet another announcement about a new idea for schools from the government – the National Literacy Strategy or synthetic phonics or SATs or the Early Years Curriculum. It all seems very complicated. It's enough to throw anyone into confusion and wonder what's best for his or her own child.

This book is just for you. Its aim is to show you how you can help a young child with literacy. It is for people who use English, whether or not it is their first language. It explains all the jargon and gives you lots of ideas for activities that are fun, as well as useful. Most of all, it will give you the confidence you need to begin! It won't take you long to realize that you are exactly the right person to help your child with literacy.

About this book

He or she?

It goes without saying that your child is either a boy or a girl! Rather than say 'he or she' each time in the book, which is very tedious, sometimes 'he' is used and sometimes 'she'.

Key to the symbols

 This indicates a **good idea**. These are mostly activities that will add variety to the time you spend helping your child.

 This indicates things to **watch out** for! Lots of children have exactly the same problems. With these tips, you can be one step ahead!

 When a technical term is used, you might think '**What's this?**' Words are explained immediately, so you don't have to spend time turning to the Glossary on page 49, where all the terms are listed.

What you can do to help

Choose a good place

Whether in school or at home perhaps you could have a special place where you work together. The best sort of place would be:

■ Quiet

■ Comfortable

■ Uncluttered

Make sure you have everything you need there.

Why not ask your child to help you to choose a corner, and set it up? It would be great if you could keep the same place all the time.

Choose a good time

If possible make it when you're not tired or rushed!

Definitely choose a time when your child is not:

■ Tired, hungry or unwell

■ Wanting to watch a favourite TV programme

Choosing the time together would be best.

Don't make it a long session. Ten minutes? Fifteen minutes? See how it goes! You're the best person to judge. A short session each day works better than a long one once a week.

Be clear about what you're doing

Have two or three small tasks ready in advance for each session. Begin by talking about them and decide together which will be first.

You could have a 'start' and a 'finish' box. Take each task out of the 'start box' and put it in the 'finish box' once it's been completed. This gives a great sense of achievement and a clear indication that the session is moving on.

Be creative

Include games and fun activities in the tasks. It doesn't always have to be plain old reading and writing exercises. There are lots of ideas for you in the rest of this book. You'll enjoy the variety more too!

Be positive

Start and end with success. There is always, *always* something to praise in anyone's work. Of course there will be things that could be improved but finding them together is a great opportunity. It's not necessary to pick out every single mistake a child makes. Encouragement makes learning a good experience. Continual criticism makes it painful and most children will give up trying after a while.

Work together

- With your child
- With your child's teacher

There are different ways of doing everything. Almost certainly methods will have changed since you were at school. It's best for your child to work in the same way at home as at school. Ask your child how to carry out a task! Ask the teacher if both of you get stuck. You probably had a close relationship with the adults at your child's nursery or playgroup. It would be very helpful for everyone, particularly your child, if you kept this up with the school teachers as well.

Teach by example

Do it yourself and talk about it! You read and write for a
reason; sometimes just because you enjoy it and
sometimes because you need to find something out, or
pass on information to another person. Your child will
love to copy you.

All about literacy in schools

The National Literacy Strategy

The National Literacy Strategy (NLS) was launched in July 1997, by the government. It meets the general requirements of English as a subject area in the National Curriculum, but adds a lot more detail. Since 1997 it has been reviewed and developed. Its purpose is to raise standards of literacy in primary schools in England. In England it is statutory. In Wales, some areas choose to follow it. In Scotland and Northern Ireland the education systems are different.

There is a numeracy strategy too. In 2005, the numeracy and literacy strategies were named as one, the **Primary National Strategy** to bring together the approaches to the two subjects.

If you are concerned about numeracy, as well as literacy, then have a look at *Help Your Child with Numeracy* by Rosemary Russell (Continuum 2007).

All the primary school teachers have access to a **Primary Framework** for the teaching of literacy and mathematics. This sets out what the pupils should be taught in each term of their time in primary school. The children *do* learn the proper terms to describe what they are doing – like onomatopoeia! Many of the words you may come across when helping your child with literacy are explained so don't panic! Look at page 49 for the jargon-busting Glossary of terms. Just because you don't know the technical vocabulary it does not, repeat NOT, mean you can't help your child. You are the very best person – the person who can make the most difference.

Literacy Hour

Teachers have to give a daily English lesson. This is called the Literacy Hour. It has a set structure, which starts with the teacher explaining the purpose of the lesson.

The teacher demonstrates reading and writing tasks to the whole class, and concentrates on specific points.

Next the children work individually or in small groups, practising the skills they have just been shown.

At the end there is a **Plenary Session**, when the pupils discuss what they have learnt.

Learning in the Literacy Hour is structured to progress from:

Shared reading or writing – where the teacher demonstrates a skill and the children watch and learn

to

Guided reading or writing – where, in small groups, the skill is put into practice, with enough support and encouragement to help each child to be successful

to

Independent reading or writing – where the child is confident enough to work alone using the newly mastered skill

to

Plenary – discussing the lesson and celebrating success.

 Follow this pattern when you help your own child.

The years that your child is at nursery and primary school are divided into three stages.

Stage	School year	Child's age
Foundation	Pre-school and Reception	3 to 5
Key Stage 1	1 and 2	5 to 7
Key Stage 2	3 to 6	7 to 11

Attainment targets and levels

To measure the progress of your child at school, each subject is divided into different levels. English, taught at primary schools using the framework set out in the Primary National Strategy, has eight levels.

An *average ability child* is expected to have gained

■ Level 2 at the end of Key Stage 1

■ Level 4 at the end of Key Stage 2

Look at page 53 if you want to see the levels for reading and writing.

The Primary National Strategy has Literacy Learning Objectives for each school year, which are meant to help each child achieve the required level.

The table on page 10 shows what can be expected in three different areas of literacy for an average child from age 3 to 11.

Please remember that this is only a rough guide. All children are different and progress at different rates. If your child has special educational needs, these levels are not helpful. What is important is that *progress is being made*, not that your child is at the 'right' level.

Skill	Foundation Age 3–5	Key Stage 1 Age 5–7	Key Stage 2 Age 7–11
Reading words	Links sounds to letters. Reads some simple, familiar words.	Reads longer words including simple two- and three-syllable words, for example *yesterday*. Uses phonics to read unknown or difficult words. Uses context and knowledge of spoken language to predict words.	Reads independently using phonics to decode unknown words. Recognizes a range of prefixes and suffixes and how they modify meaning. Uses knowledge of words and their roots to work out the meaning of words in context.
Writing sentences	Writes own name, labels and captions. Begins to form simple sentences, sometimes using punctuation.	Composes and writes simple sentences independently to communicate meaning. Uses capital letters, and full stops to punctuate simple sentences.	Writes simple and compound sentences using nouns, verbs, adjectives and adverbs. Uses tense consistently (present, past and imperative). Uses question marks, commas, apostrophes and speech marks accurately.
Hand-writing	Holds a pencil effectively. Uses it to form recognizable letters.	Writes most letters, correctly formed and orientated. Writes with spaces between words. Uses upper-case and lower-case letters.	Uses writing that is consistent in size and spacing. Writes with neat, legible and joined handwriting.

In order to check that your child is making progress in English and Maths, the government introduced tests at the end of Key Stage 1 when your child is about 7 years old, and at the end of Key Stage 2, when your child is about 11. (Science is also tested at this time.) These tests are called **SATs (Standard Attainment Tests)**.

Should you, as a parent or carer, worry about them? Absolutely not! All too soon at secondary school, your child will be caught up in exams. That sort of pressure for a younger child is to be avoided at all costs. SATs are simply checks to see how much your child has learnt, mainly for the purposes of government statistics, not something a child can pass or fail.

Literacy at home

When should we start?

When is the right time to start your child on reading and writing? There are two possible answers to this. You could say, 'It's never too early!' or you could say, 'When she's ready!' Both these answers are right in their own way. It's never too early to talk, to play, to share books with your child, to sing nursery rhymes together – all activities that will help with literacy in the future. Very small children, however, are simply not ready for formal teaching. To try it will make them anxious and will probably hold them

Einstein's Theory of Relativity

13

back, rather than move them forward. It's rather like potty training. You could spend months and months struggling and getting upset and, worse still, upsetting your child if you start too early. If you leave it until your child is ready it could happen overnight (well almost!).

Literacy is no different. Follow the lead of your child – if he's curious about words, pointing them out, attempting to read them, then that's a perfect time to start more formal learning. If he's picking up a pencil and trying to spell his name, then that's a good starting point for writing.

What's first?

First is talking! Your adult skills with language will be transferred to your child through speaking to him, and listening to him when he talks to you. In this way he'll become familiar with thousands of words, what they mean and how to use them. It's such an important part of literacy, but it tends to be forgotten in the rush to read and write.

Having conversations with your child at every opportunity is the very best start you can give him.

What's next?

In the rest of the book we'll look in detail at reading and writing and how you can help your child. We'll look at each skill separately but remember **they are closely connected**, so whatever you do in one area will help with the others too.

Reading

There are lots of different theories about the best way to teach reading, the best way to learn. Some schools may use a particular method, but it is widely accepted that the most successful approach is to learn a whole range of strategies. Together these will support and reinforce each other, giving maximum opportunity for success. If a child finds one method tricky, another can be brought into play. We, as adults, use all the strategies without even being aware that we do. Some of them come naturally, but others have to be taught, and this is where you can help your child.

Making sense of reading

Knowing the context

Looking at the picture, and knowing that the book is about a certain subject, we have a hunch about what the words might say.

Knowing the alphabet

We recognize the letters that make up the words.

Knowing about phonics

Looking at the letters in the words, we know that those letters together make a particular sound when said out loud.

Knowing about grammar

From talking, we know that words come in a certain order in sentences. This helps us to predict what unfamiliar words might be.

Knowing words

We have a sight vocabulary, so we automatically recognize words, without having to look at the letters that make them up.

Knowing about graphics

We can spell lots of words and know that some letters in combination appear in other words too.

All books for young children contain pictures. Books for toddlers may contain no text at all, but sharing those with your child is still a learning opportunity – even holding the book the right way up! Look at the cover and the title and turn the pages from the beginning to the end of the book. Talk together about what you see and ask questions. All these things help children to develop enjoyment and an understanding of the process of reading.

When children are very young, they see words in the same way as they see pictures – as squiggly patterns and shapes, not as letters that make up a word. Words appear like this:

A child may recognize a familiar word simply by its shape on the page. That's fine when he only looks at a few words, but as he uses more words, this method won't be very helpful to him.

Another way a young child may identify a word is by noticing something particular about the way it looks. Here are some real examples.

It's easy to see that these children will very soon run into difficulties! (Think about the words 'small', 'mission' and 'moon'.)

Many children can identify a few words, with no need for picture clues, long before they start to read. They don't have to know the alphabet or the sound that each letter makes. All they have to do is remember what they've been told or what they've experienced. Most children can recognize a McDonald's sign and say it out loud, as though they are reading the word. They can say Tesco when they see the word on the carrier bag or Spaghetti Hoops when they see the tin.

 Your child may be remembering, which is great, but it's not reading.

It's the same with books that your child reads over and over again. Your child *looks* and *sounds* as though he's reading the words on the page but . . . you've guessed it . . . he may only be remembering them. It doesn't matter at all, but you need to be able to tell the difference, otherwise it will be difficult to help your child to progress.

A child will gradually learn that pictures and words are different – that words are symbols that communicate a meaning. Single words under pictures are a first step towards reading. Children are very good at using pictures to tell them what the word says.

Warning A child may not read a word under a picture at all. He may see a picture of a fish, point at the word and guess that it says fish. Often he will be right, but not always!

As your child reads more complicated books he will not be able to guess the words by looking at the pictures, but pictures can give a good idea about what the words might be saying.

It's a great idea to look at a book yourself, before your child starts reading it. When you're familiar with it, you can talk about the story to give an idea of what to expect, and even pick out tricky words in advance.

Label items in your house (table, door, fridge, etc.). Don't forget to write the labels in lower-case letters – television not TELEVISION – because this is the print most often found in books.

Play the Muddly Game! Swap round all the labels and get your child to put them back in the right place. (This way you'll be sure he's *reading* not remembering.)

Snack-Attack! When it's time for a snack or a drink give your child a selection, written down on cards, to choose from. Put in silly words like 'elephant' too! Start with only two cards and increase the choice as the days go by.

My Very Own Book. Make an album together using photos of familiar people, pets and places. Write the labels for the pictures separately on cards. Use Velcro© fixers so your child can add and remove them lots of times.

Phonics – not as tricky as it sounds!

Years of research has concluded that the most effective way to learn phonic skills is to be able to identify the sounds *first* then to go on to learn how these are represented in letters.

Phonics is the study of the link between letters and sounds. We see the letter S, for example, and we know the sound it makes when we say it. Or, to look at it another way, we hear the sound S and know that to write it, we use the letter S.

Name that sound!
Make a set of cards with the letters of the alphabet on them. Give your child some cards. Two or three will be quite enough to start with. Make the sound of a letter for your child to match with a card. Talk about the sound! Make it together in lots of different ways – loudly, softly, sadly, angrily.

Synthetic Phonics is much in the news lately as a recommended approach to learning to read. It means 'building up a word from its separate sounds'. 'Cat' would be built up from the sounds /c/ and /at/.

Analytical Phonics makes use of each letter to build up a word. 'Cat' would be built up from /c/ /a/ and /t/.

In the English alphabet, there are 26 letters. Most of these are **consonants**.

Five* letters of the alphabet are called **vowels**. These are **A**, **E**, **I**, **O** and **U**.

A *consonant* is a sound and the letter that represents it. You use part of your mouth to alter the flow of air to make the sound. For example, when you say /m/ you use your lips. When you say /l/ you use your tongue.

A *vowel* is a sound made only by changing the shape of your mouth when the air comes out. Try it and see!

---

* **Y** can be a vowel (e.g. happ**y**) or a consonant (e.g. **y**ellow).

So – there are 26 letters in the alphabet? So far so good! BUT . . .

In the English language there are 44 *sounds* that we use when we talk, joined together to make words. There are not enough letters in the alphabet for this, so some of the sounds are represented by two or three letters stuck together, like the sounds /sh/ and /air/.

? A *phoneme* is the technical name for a single sound in language. It can be just one letter or a combination of letters.

? A *grapheme* is the technical name for the letters and letter combinations that spell a phoneme.

? To *blend* is the process of combining phonemes to make up a bigger chunk of a word. Blend together /s/ and /tr/, for example, and you get /str/, which is the beginning of lots of words.

Oh no!

The same sound can be spelt in more than one way!

Take the phoneme /j/, which you use at the beginning of the word *jam*. Now think about the word *giant*. And what about *large*? And, worse still, *judge*, which has TWO /j/ phonemes, spelt in different ways.

The same spelling may represent more than one sound!

ea in the word t**ea**ch makes the phoneme /ee/

ea in the word br**ea**d makes the phoneme /e/

(Don't panic! See page 57 for all the phonemes/ graphemes in the English language.)

Have phonic snacks! Bananas for /b/, chocolate for /ch/, mango for /m/, sweets for /ee/.

Photocopy and ENLARGE examples of text and use felt tip pens of different colours to mark the graphemes you are learning about.

You know what interests your child – scary monsters or ponies, dinosaurs or break-dancing, it doesn't matter what. Collect any reading material you can find and use it for practice.

Felt tip marker

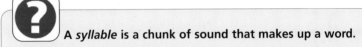

Use your child's favourite pop songs to listen for phonemes (although the words would need to be clear).

You could write down the words beforehand so your child can be reading and listening at the same time.

Oh no, NO, NO!

Surely there's no *more* to learn about phonics?

Oh yes there is!

A *syllable* is a chunk of sound that makes up a word.

Car is a word with 1 syllable.

Taxi is a word with 2 syllables (tax/i).

Syllable is a word with 3 syllables! (syll/a/ble)

Many syllables and words have what is called an **onset**.

The *onset* is the consonant or consonant cluster at the beginning, like: *b*read; *c*an; *sl*ow.

Some words and syllables have no onset, like: ear; on; under.

Syllables and words also have a **rime**.*

---

* Rime is different from the word rhyme!
Rimes (the /og/ in d**og**, l**og**, fr**og**) sound and look alike.
Rhymes (care, fair, there) sound alike but do not always look alike.

? The *rime* is the vowel and the final consonant or consonant cluster if there is one, like: the /og/ in d**og**; the /ight/ in l**ight**; the /eed/ in s**eed**.

Some words are made up of just a rime, and no onset, like: and; eel; at.

Each onset or rime appears in lots of words so if your child learns the rime /ate/ from the word gate, think how many other words she'll be able to read by adding different onsets!

L**ate**, f**ate**, m**ate**, h**ate**, cr**ate**, st**ate** . . . lots more too.

Think of all your child's friends and clap as you say their names to see how many syllables each one has. (Remember, it's important to be able to *hear* the sounds that make up words.)

The Stairs Game! Choose a rime. Start at the bottom. Go up one step for every word you think of with the same rime. How far up can you get?

The Lists Game! Choose a subject: girls' names, countries, birds, pop groups – it doesn't matter; let your child choose. Then select an onset and find as many words as you can for your subject. You could write them down too.

The Alliteration Game!

? Alliteration is the repetition of onsets.

'Big bad bunnies buy butter beans.' 'Clever clowns cling closely.' Make your own sentences!

So we know all about phonics. Can we read now?

A child can be taught the rules of phonics and that's a great help in both reading and spelling. What it *doesn't* help with is to *understand the meaning of the word.* This is why it is so important to use lots of different clues.

Imagine that a child knows all the phonemes and graphemes, all about onset and rime. She can read a sentence like 'The fat cat sat on the mat' by using her phonic skills. Using the same skills, she can read this sentence too: 'Pedagogical paradigms blended with e-learning environments facilitate a hybrid mode of delivery.' But what does it MEAN?*

Reading a word correctly is not the same as understanding it! She reads and understands 'The fat cat sat on the mat' using *lots* of skills:

- Remembering what she's learnt before

- Seeing the patterns in words

- Recognizing whole words just by looking at them

- Perhaps by looking at a picture next to the words

- Calling on her experience of fat, cats, sitting and mats!

---

* Your guess is as good as mine!

So – phonics is very important, but it is just a *part* of the process of reading. Many people believe that to learn to read *only* by analysing the structure of words is likely to take the fun away.

Having no fun is the *first* thing that will make your child hate reading, and the *last* thing that you want to happen!

Teaching phonics *within* reading is generally agreed to be the best of both worlds. The National Literacy Strategy sets out to do just that – a few minutes spent learning some rules, and more time practising the new skills by looking at poetry, stories, newspaper articles, adverts, jokes, comics . . . a huge variety of reading material.

Guess what – semantic cues and prediction

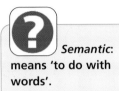

Semantic: means 'to do with words'.

When your child sees an unfamiliar word she'll use her knowledge of words – her semantic knowledge – in a variety of ways to work out what the word says.

One of those strategies is to guess! Her guess could be completely wild, but more often than not it will be determined by the use of other clues, even if she doesn't realize it at the time. The process of reading is a bit like your driving a car, when lots of skills are employed without you thinking about them.

There are lots of clues your child could use. Let's take a sentence and check it out!

He kicked the ball into the goal.

Imagine that your child does not recognize the word **goal**. What is it that might help her to guess the word correctly?

Simple clues:

1 She's reading a book about football.

2 The sentence is under a picture of a footballer scoring a penalty.

3 She loves football so knows all the relevant vocabulary.

4 She's been able to read 'He kicked the ball into the . . .'

. . . so she guesses that the word is **goal**. That was an intelligent guess! She's scored! . . . or has she?

> ⚠ **Warning** Correct guesses can be misleading. If you show your child the word *goal* all on its own, even after she has correctly guessed it, she may not be able to read it. She has relied on all the clues, but not on reading the word itself.

There are other more advanced strategies that help your child to guess a word.

Advanced clues:

1 She knows how sentences are built up, so she knows that the word must be a **noun** (a word that names an object). It wouldn't make sense if there were a **verb** (a doing word) there: 'He kicked the ball into the **going**', or an **adjective** (a describing word): 'He kicked the ball into the **good**'.

2 She has read and understood the previous sentence: 'He ran to the ball on the spot', so can predict what will happen next.

3 She has read further on and understands the next sentence, which is 'The people all clapped and he was happy.' Now she can go back to the previous sentence and guess that the unfamiliar word is **goal**.

Now you know all these strategies, if your child guesses *incorrectly* you have a great chance of helping her.

Try not to say, 'That's wrong!' Say instead, 'Does that make sense?' or 'Did that sound right?' or 'Why don't you read on and then go back to that word to see if you change your mind?'

You can help your child go beyond guessing too. If you suspect she's guessed a word, talk about it to increase her chances of knowing it next time. Say things like, 'That's great! Look at the first letter. What sound does it make? What about the last letter?'

Write some silly sentences for your child to read using a word that may be misread when guessed. For example:

- She went to school in the *cat*.
- It was cold so John put on his *goat*.
- Mum was *moving* the lawn.
- Dad washed the *fishes* after tea.

It will really show that your child is reading, not just guessing, if she gets them right. And it'll make her laugh too!

Cover up one word in a sentence and have a guessing game! When she's made her guess, reveal the word and ask if she's right, and how she knows she's right.

Here's another cunning plan!

Learning High Frequency Words

When your child is at the early stages of reading, there are certain words that will occur time and time again. In the National Literacy Strategy, these words have been identified and are called High Frequency Words. The first set of words for children just starting out is:

I	go	come	went	up	you	day	was
look	are	the	of	we	this	dog	me
like	going	big	she	and	they	my	see
on	away	mum	it	at	play	no	yes
for	a	dad	can	he	am	all	
is	cat	get	said	to	in		

Ask at your child's school for more if you need them.
Learn these together and get a head start in reading!

Dictionary delight

When you're reading together, you're sure to come across words your child doesn't know. Rather than tell him what they mean, have an up-to-date dictionary to hand. This way, he can learn to be independent – to know how to help himself when he gets stuck on a word's meaning. There are lovely dictionaries available especially for children, some with illustrations (see page 59 for a list of suggestions). Celebrate the wonder of words with your child!

Word race – give your child a list of five words to look up and time him.

My Very Own Picture Dictionary – encourage your child to make his own dictionary in a scrapbook, illustrating the words with pictures from magazines, or those he's drawn himself.

Library laughs

There was a time when libraries were serious places where everyone spoke in whispers. Not any more! Libraries are bright and cheerful places where children are welcomed. They often hold story readings and other activities for fun. Borrowing books is free!

Join your local library. Make it a regular outing with your child. Let her choose her own books!

Last words about reading

If you do nothing else, read new stories and reread old stories together whenever you can – and make it a special, happy time for both of you.

At the same time as learning to read, your child will be learning to write. Lots of the activities will overlap, but here's some information especially to do with writing.

Writing

CARDIFF
CAERDYDD

In the past, young schoolchildren seemed to spend a lot of time making zigzags and wavy lines on paper, and copying letter shapes over and over again until they were perfect. Neat writing and correct spelling had a lot more importance attached to them than the imaginative story a child was telling.

More recently, the fashion swung the other way, and spelling and handwriting were less often corrected, as long as the story was good.

Today's thinking is to take the best bits of the two approaches. Children are taught the mechanics of producing handwriting that can be read. (Using a keyboard and a computer is writing too!) At the same time, children are inspired to put these skills into practice in every sort of writing you can imagine – stories, poems, diaries, letters, lists, newspaper reports . . .

Making sense of writing

Before your child writes his first best-selling novel, there are certain things he needs to master!

- The physical process of writing – It might seem a silly question, but does he know how to hold a pencil? Lots of writing these days will be done on a computer, so keyboard skills are important too, although not dealt with in this book.

- Handwriting – Can you read what your child has written?

- Spelling – Spelling mistakes aren't the end of the world, but can put your child at a disadvantage in the future.

First things first

. . . even before picking up a pencil to write.

Very young children need lots of practice in using their hands for tasks that involve small movements. They also need to strengthen the muscles that they will use to hold a pencil.

Lots of different play activities will help them and they'll learn without even noticing.

Warning

What *won't* help is to sit a child down and make him use a pencil 'properly' before his hand is ready for it.

Playing with dough and clay

Squishing and squashing a soft squeezable toy

Using tweezers to pick up tiny objects

Pinning clothes pegs (the sort with a spring) onto the side of a box

Finger rhymes and finger puppets

Having fun!

Long before your child starts to write, he will enjoy using pencils and crayons. It's a brilliant way to learn the skill without the extra worry of forming letters correctly.

 Colouring-in books can be very frustrating. The areas to be filled in are often too tiny for someone just learning to hold a crayon. Think BIG at first!

- Use HUGE blank pieces of paper and ENORMOUS crayons to work with freely.

- Use CHUBBY chalks on a blackboard or a smooth bit of pavement. (Have fun washing it off together afterwards!)

- Use FAT marker pens on an easel or dry-wipe board.

Get washable, water-based, non-toxic pens.

Talk about the movements he makes – round and round; straight; up and down; curly; zigzag – all this will help his knowledge of the words you may use when explaining how to form letters at a later stage.

At first, your child might switch the hand that he uses.

 Don't worry!

It's not at all unusual. He'll find out which hand he prefers to use in his own time.

Warning About 10 per cent of the population is left-handed. You need to be aware if your child is left-handed. It will be trickier for him to write from left to right, so your encouragement will be even more important.

Your child might hold the pencil in an odd way.

In the beginning it's not that serious, but when he has to write a lot in school, holding a pencil incorrectly might slow him up and even cause pain in his hand, so it's a good idea to master the best way of holding before this time. It's generally agreed that this is the 'tripod grasp'.

 The **'tripod grasp'** – the pencil is supported by the thumb, index and middle finger. The ring and little finger are bent and rest comfortably on the table.

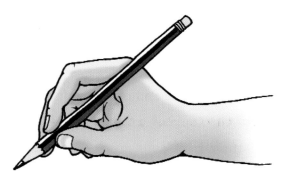

If your child has difficulty with the tripod grasp you can buy:

- Special grips that fit on to pencils

- Pencils and crayons that are triangular and easier to hold correctly

At first:

- Use BIG pencils – they too are easier to hold.

- Use SOFT pencils – you need less pressure to make a mark.

Forming letters

Practise this without even picking up a pencil.

Make the shape of letters:

- In the air with huge arm movements
- On each other's backs with a finger (Can you guess which letter it is?)
- In sand or salt in a tray
- On the pavement with chalk
- On the floor with brightly coloured sticky-tape so you can 'walk the shape'
- With pastry and play-dough
- With foam on a smooth surface

All these large-scale activities will help your child to develop a deep understanding of letter formation that he'll be able to transfer to his writing at a later stage.

Writing at last!

The next stage is to form letters on paper, with a pencil or crayon.

Still think BIG at first, so your child doesn't get anxious about writing. Only when he's learnt how to form letters correctly should you

Warning
Concentrate on lower-case letters – your child will be reading these mainly. But all children like to write their own name, so you'll need to explain about capital letters for this purpose.

begin to encourage him to reduce the size.

And only then should you introduce the idea of writing along a line.

Always encourage working from LEFT TO RIGHT, in the same way as we read.

Tracing over dot-to-dot letters can help your child to form letters correctly but is not at all exciting. Don't do it very much!

Play noughts and crosses, using two letters that you're practising instead of a O and a X.

Play hangman, writing the letter that is your guess instead of saying it.

Choose a 'letter of the day' and think of lots of things to do as well as writing it.

Make your own lined paper together, using a ruler. Be sure the lines are widely spaced to begin with.

Cursive writing or printing?

Children generally start with printing but it's much slower than cursive writing. Your child's school should have a handwriting policy in which the agreed style will be set out.

Cursive writing simply means joined-up writing, whereas *printing* is writing the letters individually.

Find out what's happening at school.

Encourage your child to *read* cursive writing.

Practise cursive writing with onsets and rimes (see page 24).

Writing for a purpose

Writing exercises are helpful to learn a specific skill, but your child needs to see how *useful* it is to write – and he'll probably be bursting to get on with something that has a purpose, especially something that will help *you*.

 Get your child involved in simple writing tasks:

- **Shopping or 'to do' lists**
- **Notes to other members of the family**
- **Phone messages**
- **Holiday postcards**
- **Invitations and greetings cards**
- **Appointments in your diary or on the calendar**

Spelling

Is it really that important? For your child's future – yes it is! Even today, when word processors with spell-checkers are so widely used, there are still times when we need to write by hand.

Poor spelling creates a bad impression in exams and for prospective employers BUT

> ⚠️ **Warning** Anxiety about spelling may inhibit your child's writing, making her frightened to use new words in case she makes a mistake.

That's where you can help so much. You can make her feel safe about trying new words without fear of criticism.

Exactly in the same way as learning to read, for spelling it's useful to know:

- How words are built up

- The patterns that occur in many words

- Common beginnings and endings – which, in this context, are known as:

Prefixes and suffixes

Look at the word *appear*. This word can stand alone, but we can change its meaning by adding to it.

Add /dis/ at the beginning and we get **dis**appear.

Add /ed/ at the end and we get appear**ed**.

There are other variations – appear**ance**, appear**ing**, appear**s**.

? An addition at the beginning of a word that changes its meaning is known as a *prefix*.

? An addition at the end of a word that changes its meaning is known as a *suffix*.

What's this got to do with spelling? If your child knows how to spell all the common prefixes and suffixes, then she'll be able to add these to many basic words and increase her spelling vocabulary many times over!

Check back on your work with onset and rime on page 25. There you'll find common word patterns.

Look at the High Frequency Words on pages 31–2. Knowing how to spell these is very helpful too.

But don't forget to have FUN!

Make your own spelling book together. Have a page for each letter of the alphabet, and encourage your child to write down each new word she's learnt to spell.

Spell words incorrectly on purpose, and ask your child to correct them.

Spelling countdown. Have a list of ten words to spell, numbered like a rocket countdown (10, 9, 8, etc.). Spell each word in turn, saying the number too – make it dramatic! When you get to zero leap up like a rocket launching! It would be a great way to end a session.

Talk together spelling out words: 'Would you like to go to the p-a-r-k?' 'There's a present for you in your c-u-p-b-o-a-r-d.'

Punctuation and grammar

? *Punctuation* is a way of marking text to help the readers' understanding. It includes full stops, commas, question marks, apostrophes and exclamation marks.

? *Grammar* is the study of how words combine to form sentences.

Correct use of punctuation and grammar in writing also creates a good impression. It makes your child's work easy to read, so that whatever she wants to say will be communicated. There are many books available to help out if you're not sure about it. See the list of suggestions on page 59.

A great way to learn about these aspects of writing is by reading. All the rules will become familiar just by seeing them over and over again, almost without your child noticing what's happening.

What to write

Oh what beautiful handwriting and perfect spelling! But what does it SAY? Does it make sense? Is it interesting?

It's not necessary to have beautiful handwriting, perfect spelling, grammar and punctuation in order to write a thrilling story, or a sad poem or an interesting news item. It would be terrible for your child to feel that he couldn't write freely just in case he made a mistake. When your child reaches the stage of exams, all the mechanics of writing are important, so that ideas can be communicated effectively, but creativity must be encouraged too.

It's *up to you* to be very clear about the purpose of each writing exercise. Is your child practising handwriting? Then *don't* correct every last spelling mistake. Is he working on creating an adventure story? Then *don't* worry if the writing is a bit messy.

Deal with those sorts of problems separately.

Sometimes, when your child wants to tell a story, *you* write down what he says, then read it back together.

Don't be dull!

Writing stories? Encourage the use of exciting language in your child's work.

Silly Similes – choose a word and make a simile . . . He was as thin as a . . . She ran like a . . .

The Instead of Said Game! – make a sentence like 'It's very cold today,' she said. Then choose as many words as you can think of to use Instead of Said and act them out! 'It's very cold today,' she shouted, she whispered, she whined . . .

A *simile* is a comparison between two things: He was as cold as an icicle. She sings like a nightingale.

Sounds like? – get together a selection of objects – tins and saucepans, brushes and scissors, paper to crumple and water to splash. Make the noise, then think of a word that would describe it. Use the word in a story!

This is *onomatopoeia* – the use of a word that sounds like the noise . . . the *snip* of scissors, the *swish* of a brush.

No, definitely don't be dull!

Don't stick to stories . . . plan a play . . . jot in a journal . . . dictate a diary . . . pen a poem . . . write a report . . . create a commercial . . . fill in a form . . .

And finally . . . enjoy yourselves!

Glossary

Listed below are all the specialist terms that are used in this book.

You can find a complete glossary of words to do with literacy at: http://www.standards.dfes.gov.uk/primary/publications/literacy/63285/
You can download this document for your reference.

Adjective
A word that describes somebody or something: The **big** dog; I am **happy**; **horrible** weather.

Alliteration
A series of words that start with the same sound:
Moaning **M**ary **M**iller **r**an **r**ight **r**ound the **r**osebush.

Analytical Phonics
Uses the sound of each letter to build up a word. 'Bus' would be built up from **/b/ /u/** and **/s/**.

Blend
To combine *phonemes* into larger group such as *syllables* and words: **/ch/** + **/ea/** + **/t/** blend together to make the word **cheat**. A group of two or more *phonemes* is also called a *blend*; for example: **/str/ /pl/ /nd/**.

Consonant
A speech sound made by obstructing the airflow with part of your mouth. Also, the letter that represents that sound. The sound **/t/** is made using the tip of your tongue; the sound **/f/** is made using your teeth on your lips.

Cursive writing
Joined-up writing, as opposed to printing.

Grammar
The study of how words combine to form sentences.

Grapheme
The written letters that represent a sound. Could be just one letter or a group. The sound /**n**/ can be made by /**n**/ as in **n**o, or /**kn**/ as in **kn**ife or /**gn**/ as in **gn**ome (see page 57 for a complete list).

Lower-case letters
'Little' letters as opposed to capital, or upper-case letters.

Noun
A word that represents somebody or something: Mother; paper; house; dog; lottery.

Onomatopoeia
The use of a word which sounds like its meaning: Hiss; pop; bubbling; swish.

Onset
The initial consonant or group of consonants: /**c**/at; /**cl**/atter; /**tr**/iangle; /**pl**/ate.

Phoneme
The name for a single sound in language. It can be just one letter or a combination of letters (see page 57 for a complete list).

Phonics
The study of the link between letters and sounds.

Plenary
In the Literacy Hour – an opportunity to round off and summarize the lesson, to underline what has been accomplished.

Portmanteau word
A word made from a combination of two words. Smoke combined with fog = smog.

Prefix
An addition at the beginning of a word that changes its meaning. For example, take the word **manageable**. Put the prefix **/un/** at the beginning and you get **unmanageable**.

Printing
Writing each letter separately.

Punctuation
A way of marking text to help the readers' understanding. It includes full stops, commas, question marks, apostrophes and exclamation marks.

Rhyme
A word that sounds like another but may not look alike.

Rime
In a word – the vowel and the final consonant or consonant cluster if there is one, like: the **/og/** in dog.

SATs – Standard Attainment Tests
Carried out nationally at ages 7, 11 and 14, covering English, Maths and Science.

Semantic
To do with language.

Simile

A comparison between two different things: 'Jane is as cool as a cucumber.'

Suffix

An addition at the end of a word that changes its meaning. For example, take the word **manage**. Add the suffix /**able**/ and you get **manageable**.

Syllable

A chunk of sound in a word. Dog has one syllable, baby two and bicycle three.

Synthetic Phonics

To build up a word from its separate sounds. 'Jam' would be built up from the sounds /**j**/ and /**am**/.

Tripod grasp

Generally agreed to be the best way to hold a pencil. The pencil is supported by the thumb, index and middle finger. The ring and little finger are bent and rest comfortably on the table.

Upper-case letters

'Big' or capital letters.

Verb

A 'doing' or 'being' word that describes an action, a happening or a state. 'Jamie is hungry and wants to go to the café.' **Is**, **wants** and **go** are the verbs.

Vowel

A sound made simply by changing the shape of your mouth as the air comes out, and the letter that represents this. **A**, **E**, **I**, **O** and **U** are the major vowels.

Reading and writing levels

Level 1

Pupils recognize familiar words in simple texts. They use their knowledge of letters and sound–symbol relationships in order to read words and to establish meaning when reading aloud. In these activities they sometimes require support. They express their response to poems, stories and non-fiction by identifying aspects they like.

Level 2

Pupils' reading of simple texts shows understanding and is generally accurate. They express opinions about major events or ideas in stories, poems and non-fiction. They use more than one strategy, such as phonic, graphic, syntactic and contextual, in reading unfamiliar words and establishing meaning.

Level 3

Pupils read a range of texts fluently and accurately. They read independently, using strategies appropriately to establish meaning. In responding to fiction and non-fiction they show understanding of the main points and express preferences. They use their knowledge of the alphabet to locate books and find information.

Level 4

In responding to a range of texts, pupils show understanding of significant ideas, themes, events and characters, beginning to use inference and deduction. They refer to the text when explaining their views. They locate and use ideas and information.

Writing

Level 1

Pupils' writing communicates meaning through simple words and phrases. In their reading or their writing, pupils begin to show awareness of how full stops are used. Letters are usually clearly shaped and correctly orientated.

Level 2

Pupils' writing communicates meaning in both narrative and non-narrative forms, using appropriate and interesting vocabulary, and showing some awareness of the reader. Ideas are developed in a sequence of sentences, sometimes demarcated by capital letters and full stops. Simple, monosyllabic words are usually spelt correctly, and where there are inaccuracies the alternative is phonetically plausible. In handwriting, letters are accurately formed and consistent in size.

Level 3

Pupils' writing is often organized, imaginative and clear. The main features of different forms of writing are used appropriately, beginning to be adapted to different readers. Sequences of sentences extend ideas logically and words are chosen for variety and interest. The basic grammatical structure of sentences is usually correct.

Spelling is usually accurate, including that of common, polysyllabic words. Punctuation to mark sentences – full stops, capital letters and question marks – is used accurately. Handwriting is joined and legible.

Level 4

Pupils' writing in a range of forms is lively and thoughtful. Ideas are often sustained and developed in interesting ways and organized appropriately for the purpose of the reader. Vocabulary choices are often adventurous and words are used for effect. Pupils are beginning to use grammatically complex sentences, extending meaning. Spelling, including that of polysyllabic words that conform to regular patterns, is generally accurate. Full stops, capital letters and question marks are used correctly, and pupils are beginning to use punctuation within the sentence. Handwriting style is fluent, joined and legible.

Phonemes and graphemes

Vowel phonemes and how they are written as graphemes.

Vowel phonemes	Examples in words
/a/	man, bat
/e/	leg, head
/i/	pit, sorted
/o/	dog, want
/u/	cup, glove
/ae/	rain, play, rate, nation
/ee/	feed, beat, chief, these
/ie/	fried, night, why, time, kind
/oe/	road, know, phone, sold
/ue/	soon, blue, shoe, new, June
/oo/	book, could, put
/ar/	car, bath*
/ur/	turn, firm, stern, learn, work
/or/	born, floor, war
/au/	Paul, saw, ball
/er/	sister, garden, focus
/ow/	cow, scout
/oi/	join, toy
/air/	hair, bear, fare
/ear/	near, cheer, here

---

* In some areas of the UK bath is said with an /a/ as in man.

Consonant phonemes and how they are written as graphemes.

Consonant phonemes	Examples in words
/b/	**b**angle
/d/	**d**ish
/f/	**f**ace, **ph**one
/g/	**g**ate
/h/	**h**ouse, **wh**o
/j/	**j**am, bu**dg**et, **g**iraffe, lar**ge**
/k/	**c**at, **k**iss, **q**uit, fi**x**, li**ck**, **Ch**ristmas
/l/	**l**eg
/m/	**m**oney, la**mb**
/n/	**n**ose, **kn**ife, **gn**ome
/p/	**p**erson
/r/	**r**ed, **wr**ite
/s/	**s**oap, ba**se**, **c**ity, **sc**ien**ce**
/t/	**t**op
/v/	**v**an
/w/	**w**ish
/wh/	**wh**y
/y/	**y**ellow
/z/	**z**oo, chee**se**, hi**s**
/th/	**th**is
/th/	**th**ick
/ch/	**ch**oose, pa**tch**
/sh/	**sh**ape, permi**ssi**on, condi**ti**on, **ch**ef
/zh/	mea**s**ure
/ng/	si**ng**, pi**nk**

Useful websites and possible purchases

This is just a selection. It's best to go to a bookshop with your child, or go online and see material first-hand. You know your child better than anyone!

Children's dictionaries

Oxford University Press: A wonderful range of dictionaries for every age group. You can see this at: http://www.oup.co.uk/oxed/dictionaries/primary/

Usborne Books: *The Very First Dictionary* – for very young, pre-school children.

Collins: *A First School Dictionary* for 4- to 5-year-olds.

Grammar and punctuation

Usborne Books: *The Usborne Guide to English Grammar* and *The Usborne Guide to English Punctuation*.

Keyboard skills

CBeebies: 'You, Your Child and Technology' at: http://www.bbc.co.uk/cbeebies/grownups/children_learn/technology/

Usborne Books: *Starting Computers.*

Series of literacy books

See these in shops and sometimes online too. Bright, fun and lively!
Especially:

'Magical Skills from Letts' at:
http://shop.letts-successzone.com/icat/magicalskills

Check out:
* 'Funny Phonics and Silly Spelling'
* 'Hilarious Handwriting'

'Jolly Learning' at: http://www.jollylearning.co.uk/

Bright Start English from WHSmith.

I Can Learn from Egmont Books.

DON'T FORGET – you don't need to buy lots of practice books. They can be boring for your child, and there are plenty of activities suggested in this book that you can do at home together, using everyday materials, and what's more, they don't cost anything!

Websites

For fun with your child!

BBC Words and Pictures at:
http://www.bbc.co.uk/schools/wordsandpictures/

BBC The Little Animals Activity Centre at:
http://www.bbc.co.uk/schools/laac/

Stories from the web at:
http://www.storiesfromtheweb.org/earlyyears/sfw07_stories.asp

LearnEnglish Kids from the British Council at:
http://www.britishcouncil.org/kids.htm
– particularly useful if English is not your first language.

More information for you

The National Literacy Trust – ideas and current thinking, and the Family Reading Campaign, at:
www.literacytrust.org.uk

The Basic Skills Agency – aim to help people of all ages who struggle with words (and numbers) in their everyday lives, at: http://www.basic-skills.co.uk

Sure Start – the government programme aiming to deliver the best start in life for every child at:
http://www.surestart.gov.uk/

The Parents' Centre – helping you to help your child at:
http://www.parentscentre.gov.uk/educationandlearning/whatchildrenlearn/ – lots of information about educational matters and advice for particular needs.

Help for Left-Handed Children at:
http://www.anythingleft-handed.co.uk/kids_help.html

The British Dyslexia Association at:
http://www.bdadyslexia.org.uk/

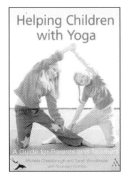